¡Dichos!

Also by Joseph J. Keenan

Breaking Out of Beginner's Spanish

THE WIT & WHIMSY *of* SPANISH SAYINGS

Joseph J. Keenan

UNIVERSITY OF TEXAS PRESS

Austin

Copyright © 2019 by the University of Texas Press
All rights reserved
First edition, 2019

Requests for permission to reproduce material from
this work should be sent to:

    Permissions
    University of Texas Press
    P.O. Box 7819
    Austin, TX 78713-7819
    utpress.utexas.edu/rp-form

♾ The paper used in this book meets the minimum requirements of
ANSI/NISO Z39.48-1992 (R1997) (Permanence of Paper).

Library of Congress Cataloging-in-Publication Data
Names: Keenan, Joseph J. (Joseph John), 1960– author.
Title: ¡Dichos! : the wit and whimsy of Spanish sayings / Joseph J. Keenan.
Description: First edition. | Austin : University of Texas Press, 2019.
Identifiers: LCCN 2018014801
 ISBN 978-1-4773-2863-7 (pbk.)
 ISBN 978-1-4773-1819-5 (library e-book)
 ISBN 978-1-4773-1820-1 (non-library e-book)
Subjects: LCSH: Proverbs, Spanish. | Spanish language—Terms and
phrases. | Spanish language—Idioms. | Proverbs, Spanish—Translations
into English.
Classification: LCC PN6491 .K44 2019 | DDC 398.9/61—dc23
LC record available at https://lccn.loc.gov/2018014801

doi:10.7560/318188

El que no oye consejo
no llega a viejo.

Contents

Las gracias

There is no way to list all the friends and strangers over all these years who have shared these expressions with me—or simply used them where I was in a position to overhear or read them. Nonetheless, to them I owe my thanks.

I owe a special thanks to Patricia Díaz de Bezaury and her husband Juan, whose love for *dichos* is as strong as their skill for spotting mistakes I made in transcribing or interpreting them.

Great thanks are also due the University of Texas Press and my editor, Jim Burr. He and his colleagues encouraged me to collect and write about these *dichos* and made the process of doing so enjoyable. A special thanks to Nancy Warrington, my venerable copy editor, who had the patience and discernment to get deep inside the *dichos* and their translations. (Sorry for the sentence fragment!)

Thanks finally and always to my three beloved "chitlins," Flavita, Andrés, and Adrián, for the constant inspiration to write down what little I've managed to learn—and then go try to learn some more.

Introduction

It's not uncommon to hear people say they "love" a language, but it's not immediately obvious what that means or why we would love one collection of words, phrases, and syntax more than another.

And yet: I love Spanish. So let me try to explain.

A language helps us frame and interpret our world. It allows us to create concepts that without it would float forever out of reach. When we find just the right words to hook the concept, we can reel it in and hold it close. The world becomes a little more familiar, explicable, and meaningful.

And—often—funnier. Words arranged in certain ways can reshape our feelings of sadness or perplexity and humanize them, making us chuckle at our bad luck or marvel at the sinuous workings of the world. Sometimes well-arranged words reach the level of "black humor," a weapon against an all-powerful universe that doesn't always seem to have our best interests in mind. And so we assemble some words in a way we call "wit," laugh knowingly or grudgingly, and trudge on.

Words, well arranged, become *dichos* and their cousins: turns of phrase that take the dust and irritants of our daily lives and mold them into little linguistic pearls. For example, I could encourage you to take advantage of a situation to generate greater benefit for yourself. Or, I could tell you to "Get stuck now while there's mud." I could tell you that things will get better, and that they could always be worse; or I could just tell you that "God didn't give wings to scorpions."

And so it is that over the years and down through the centuries, new bits of wisdom and wit have been layered on, molding messages to new generations and new realities. Sometimes these expressions arise from an innovative reformulation of an old thought, and sometimes they represent new thoughts altogether. Sometimes TV shows, musicians, or politicians (often inadvertently) bring memorable new soundbites into the culture, and sometimes the wizards of marketing do. But always, somewhere, brains and tongues are conspiring to turn phrases into pearls.

This book is a compendium of a small part of this cultural trove of wisdom and wit, old and new, gleaned from the streets and *salas* of the Spanish-speaking world. Where I know the specific origin of a *dicho*, I mention it in the text, but many *dichos'* origins are lost in the past or have sprung up spontaneously and spread virally across cultures and countries. Wit knows no borders, it seems.

Probably the greatest number of *dichos* in the book are from Mexico, or at least are used there, since that is where I have spent the most time living and listening. Many of these expressions are nearly universally recognized but appear in different forms in different places; I tried to choose the most widely used version, based loosely on total Google hits. That measure will change, and, in any case, you should listen for the local version wherever you are.

Above all, this book is a labor of love—my love for the Spanish language and, by extension, for the people who speak it and use it to make sense (and maybe a little fun) of our mixed-up modern world.

If you are a fan of language and of the magic that words can create, then this book is for you. If you are learning Spanish, these expressions will help you understand it a bit more deeply—and hopefully help you enjoy learning it. If you already are intimate with Spanish, these *dichos* may rekindle some long-ago memories. And no doubt the book will remind you of a dozen more *dichos* that are meaningful to you.

Finally, a clarification: There is a debate in academic circles about what constitutes a *dicho* as opposed to some of its cousins, like the *refranes*, *sentencias*, *proverbios*, *adagios*, *aforismos*, and others. It is an interesting debate, but I have chosen to ignore it for the purposes of this book. Here I'm calling them all *dichos*. After all, a rose by any other name . . .

A Adryana:

"mi táctica es
hablarte
y escucharte
construir con palabras
un puente indestructible."

—MARIO BENEDETTI

1. ¿Que what?

To get us started, let's look at some *dichos* that may leave you scratching your head at whether they mean what you think they say, or say what you think they mean, or . . .

Oh, forget it. Yogi Berra would've understood them.

**Ahora que se había acostumbrado a
no comer, va y se muere el burro.**

*Just when it was getting used to not
eating, my burro up and dies on me.*

Okay, so it doesn't exactly roll off the tongue, but it's
an amusing way to poke a little fun at yourself when
a neat plan of yours goes awry in a way that anyone
could have predicted—and that you probably did
yourself—before going ahead anyhow.

**A veces me siento a pensar,
y a veces nomás me siento.**

*Sometimes I sit and think,
and sometimes I just sit.*

Zen.

Eso sí que no.

Yes, that's a no.

Maybe it's just me, but this one always brings to mind the classic popular tune "Yes! We Have No Bananas." In fact, *Eso sí que no* is generally used as an emphatic way of saying "no," but thanks to its peculiar syntax, it works as a softer, fuzzier "no" as well, useful for saying "no" indirectly and thus not hurting any feelings.

(By the way, its affirmative counterpart—*Eso sí que es*—features prominently in a lame joke about a Spanish speaker trying to buy socks in New York. Say it out loud and slowly. Still don't get it? S-O-C-K-S. Oh, never mind.)

**Yo no sé si va' ser dura o blanda,
    pero blanda no va' ser.**

*I don't know if it'll be hard or easy,
    but it ain't gonna be easy.*

Country wisdom: though syntactically nonsensical, it's clear as a bell, neatly capturing a sense of the hard life.

Me clavó el puñal, pero se lo ensangrenté.

He stabbed me, but I bled on his knife.

Take that! This one's a bit like "You should see what the other guy looks like" after showing up looking worse for wear. It also expresses the black humor of the downtrodden, recognizing their overall impotence while never accepting that they can't cause the *patrón* some harm.

La operación fue un éxito,
pero el paciente se murió.

The operation was a success,
*   but the patient died.*

As a sample of double-talk—or preposterous
excuse making—it would be hard to beat this
one, and this saying is most useful precisely when
one is getting so much spin on an answer that an
ironic aside is needed to bring things back around
to reality, or closer to it at least. "So let me see,
doctor (lawyer, politician, etc.), what you're telling
me is that the operation was a success, but ... "

Así pasa cuando sucede.

That's what happens when it happens.

One of many classic lines attributed to the "Güémez Philosopher," a (probably) apocryphal folk sage from a rural Mexican village. Here are a few others:

Todo lo que sube tiende a bajar . . .
    a menos que se quede arriba.

What goes up tends to come down . . .
    unless it stays up.

Quien tenga perro,
    que lo amarre,
    y quien no . . . pues no.

Those who have a dog should
    tie it up, and those who don't . . .
    well, shouldn't.

La buena vida es cara; hay una más barata, pero no es tan buena.

The good life is expensive; there is a cheaper one, but it's not as good.

Poignant, but alas, so true. Might help to explain why the rich are different from you and me after all . . .

2. Las reglas

Next up are those *dichos* that lay out the rules of the game, how things work. This is the wisdom of ages, distilled down into soundbites that have been handed down across centuries. Sometimes they slip into finger-wagging, tut-tut, didn't-your-mama-teach-you-anything territory. But most of them are just plain common sense—which, as we all know, isn't as common as all that. (But it would be if people studied their *dichos*!)

El que mucho abarca poco aprieta.

*Those who embrace too much
squeeze too little.*

A very common and universal expression, and one
that is used to rein in the overstretched would-be
overachiever. Similar in some ways to "Jack of all
trades, master of none." (*Aprendiz de todo, maestro de
nada.*) But a good English equivalent is still waiting
to be invented: "He who bites off more than he can
chew, _____."

**No hay que llegar primero,
pero hay que saber llegar.**

*It's not about arriving first but
about knowing how to arrive.*

From the wisdom-rich world of Mexico's *ranchera*
music, this lyric *dicho* provides sound advice for
those reflective moments when we lift up our tequila
snifter, gaze out over the sawdust floor of our neighborhood cantina, and ponder life's complexities. This
proverb helps put things in their proper perspective—
or is that the tequila?

Lo cortés no quita lo valiente.

Being courteous does not diminish one's valor.

In other words, chill out! This expression is most
frequently aimed at someone who is gruff or rude in
a situation where toughness may be called for . . . but
not rudeness. Kind of an "Okay, but you don't have to
be a *jerk* about it."

Hasta no ver, no creer.

Until I see it, I won't believe it.

Attributed to St. Thomas (as "Seeing is believing"),
who wouldn't believe his fellow apostles' account of
Jesus's resurrection. Thanks to this quip, he became
the world's original "doubting Thomas."

Lo que no te mata te fortalece.

What doesn't kill you makes you stronger.

A familiar concept, courtesy originally of Nietzsche, but for some reason it is more often used in Spanish in relation to strange foods, or a piece of food that has fallen on the floor, or something that has been in the fridge just a week or two too long. These days it is quite often encountered as:

Lo que no mata engorda.

What doesn't kill you makes you fat.

To which you might respond, *Más vale morir de gordo que de hambre*—"Better to die from being fat than from hunger."

Dios no les dio alas a los alacranes.

God didn't give wings to scorpions.

A kind of roundabout and picturesque way of saying "God will provide." The idea is, as bad as you think things are, buck up! If God had really wanted to make you suffer, She would have given scorpions wings! Small comfort.

3. *El juego*

Rules are just rules, as anyone who has spent any time south of the border knows. And following the rules will only get you so far. As I've heard it explained, "One thing is the rules, another thing is the game"—*el juego*. So what are some expressions that can help guide you through the game?

Es más fácil pedir perdón que permiso.

It's easier to ask forgiveness than permission.

Asking permission, in the kinds of bureaucratic cultures that often accompany the use of the Spanish language around the globe, simply takes too damn long. Who can wait? You can always apologize later!

Siempre di que sí, nunca digas cuando.

Always say yes, never say when.

A wily way to deflect a request for a favor—or for permission. It's so much more polite than saying no, but let's face it, it works out just the same.

**Al que quiera azul celeste,
       que le cueste.**

*If you want a blue sky,
       it's gonna cost you.*

Put another way, there ain't no free lunch. You have to work hard to reach the "blue sky." This saying is also rolled out to freeze in their tracks people who make requests that go beyond the normal and the fair. Like many old sayings, this one has gained a new and more impish and irreverent variant:

**Quien quiera azul celeste,
       que se acueste.**

*Whoever wants a blue sky
       had better lie down.*

In other words, think "casting couch," a practice we hope has seen its final days.

No hagas cosas buenas que parezcan malas (ni malas que parezcan buenas).

Don't do good things that look bad (or bad things that look good).

This is a handier expression, and concept, than you might at first think—the first part especially. Helping a little old lady across the street is noble, but if you take away her purse to get a better grip on her arm, you'll be in a real pinch if she screams, "Thief!" Often invoked these days by public figures and companies, who have to be conscious not just of *what* they do but of how what they do might *look* to a social-media-energized public. Optics matter.

**Dios está en todas partes,
    pero atiende en Buenos Aires.**

*God is everywhere,
    but He does business in Buenos Aires.*

A snarky reference to how countries centralize every-thing, and to get anything done you have to go to the capital city. Useful for snarking about bureaucracies in general that require you to deal with headquarters to get things done.

La ropa sucia se lava en casa.

Dirty clothes get washed at home.

In other words, don't broadcast your troubles outside of your family, business, and so on. Instead, deal with these issues quietly and behind closed doors. Dis-cretion, after all, is the better part of valor. Clearly, however, this expression was invented by someone who never watched reality TV.

4. Ciencias políticas

When it comes to using language to convey high-sounding, inspiring, and utterly meaningless gibberish, it's hard to beat the world's politicians. Latin America is not only not the exception to this rule, it is the origin of some of the most advanced political doublespeak ever invented—and the source as well of some cynical one-liners that describe this murky world.

**Ni nos beneficia ni nos perjudica,
sino todo lo contrario.**

*It doesn't help us or hurt us,
but just the opposite.*

Said first by a Mexican president in the 1970s, this
phrase has since entered the popular lexicon as a
simple nonexplanation for pretty much everything.

**No nos dejemos vencer por los derrotistas que
quieren llenarnos de optimismo.**

*Let's not let ourselves be beaten by the defeatists
who want to fill us with optimism.*

A former Argentine president offered a similarly
mystifying assessment of his opponents.

El que no transa, no avanza.

He who doesn't cheat, doesn't get ahead.

A hard-boiled view of the world of politics, where sticking one's hands in the public coffers has come with the territory for as far back as most citizens can remember. This saying comes from Mexico, where the verb *transar* has taken on the meaning of "to cheat" or "to rip off."

Se vale meter la pata pero no la mano (en la lata).

It's okay to stick your foot in it (i.e., screw up) but not your hand (in the money jar).

The sad tradition of public officials employing the "five-finger discount" led a Mexican president back in the 1920s to issue this order to his underlings. The president in question, Álvaro Obregón, was a war hero who had lost an arm fighting in the country's revolution—leading him to declare himself to be the best candidate for president because he had only one arm to steal with!

Año de Hidalgo, chingue a su madre el que deje algo.

The year of Hidalgo, screw the fool who leaves anything behind.

In Mexico, the final year of a president's single six-year term is called the "year of Hidalgo," on the surface a reference to the country's hero of the War of Independence, Miguel Hidalgo. In fact, the real reason it's called that has to do with this mocking (and vulgar) little rhyme that presumably guides the greedy behavior of the country's public servants during their final year in power.

Todos tienen cola que les pisen.

Everyone's got a tail that can be stepped on.

In this sense, "having a tail" is much the same as having a "skeleton in the closet," and having that tail stepped on is the same as having the door to the closet thrown wide open. In other words, it can be assumed that everyone has something to hide, and the powers that be are ready to expose it at any moment to keep everyone in line.

En este país, nadie se hace rico trabajando.

In this country, no one gets rich by working.

From Argentina, a cynical view of the route from rags to riches.

Quien hizo la ley hizo la trampa.

Those who made the law made the loophole.

Also heard as "*Hecha la ley, hecha la trampa.*" The point here is that those who make the laws are the least likely to obey them, having made them in the first place in a way that they could safely ignore them.

Un político pobre es un pobre político.

*A poor (indigent) politician
    is a poor (lousy) politician.*

Attributed to a Mexican cabinet minister, this pretty much sums up the politicians' view of themselves, for what kind of politician would they be if they didn't get rich in the process?

Cuando llegué al poder, la nación estaba al borde del abismo. Desde entonces, hemos dado un gran paso hacia adelante . . .

When I took office, the country was on the edge of an abyss. Since then, we have taken a great step forward . . .

Attributed, no doubt apocryphally, to elected officials and ministers the world over. Though probably not actually of Latin American origin, it was too good to exclude!

El que se mueve no sale en la foto.

*The one who moves doesn't come out in
    the photo.*

Famously attributed to a Mexican labor boss who was
taking care not to tip his hand in the upcoming selection of a new presidential candidate. For if you move
too soon, you'll be the blurry one in the photo.

5. *Llorar y llorar*

Bad things can happen, of course. And when they do, you might as well be armed with a good *dicho*. For human nature's dark side is by no means immune to the curative power of the *dicho*.

Using *dichos* in these situations is not likely to solve your problems, but you might just feel wiser as you gaze into the gaping maw of your rotten luck.

No vale nada la vida/
   La vida no vale nada/
   Comienza siempre llorando/
   Y así llorando se acaba

Worth nothing is life/
   Life is worth nothing/
   It always starts with crying/
   and crying is how it ends

These opening lines of the classic Mexican *ranchera* song ("Camino de Guanajuato") could pass for the saddest of all laments. No one here gets out alive, after all.

La vida es una pendejada, y lo demás es
   consecuencia de la misma.

Life is a bowl of crap, and everything else is a
   consequence of that.

So . . . life's a bitch and then you die?

**Dios, cuídame de mis amigos,
que de mis enemigos me cuido yo.**

*God, protect me from my friends;
I can handle my enemies myself.*

A cynical statement on friendship, suggesting that
friends are even less trustworthy than enemies, since
at least your enemies are transparent about their
intentions.

Piensa mal y acertarás.

Think poorly (of someone) and you'll be right.

If cynicism can be defined as always expecting the
worst from fellow humans, then its slogan could
easily be this dire but very commonly heard piece of
proverbial advice.

El que no corre, vuela.

The one that doesn't run, flies.

Brings to mind the English expression, "Still waters run deep." This is advice to keep an eye on the slow/quiet ones, the ones you might least expect anything from, because they may end up surprising you by "flying." Also used more generically to tell you to stay on your toes, suggesting each one (in a particular place or situation) is slicker and sneakier than the next guy. *Cuidado, por aquí el que no corre, vuela* ("Careful, around here you gotta watch yourself").

Perdonamos todo menos el éxito ajeno.

We can forgive anything except another's success.

A clever proverb that pokes a little fun at itself, and at all fellow humans, while making a point about how we loathe to see others get ahead.

Qué bonito es ver llover y no mojarse.

How great it is to watch it rain and not get wet.

On the other hand, witnessing hardship without experiencing it oneself can bring a certain grim pleasure. Possibly the best Spanish translation of *Schadenfreude*.

It is often used to put down the armchair or sideline critic, who never attempts to do something him or herself but enjoys criticizing how others do it.

6. Macho, macho men

Latin American culture is certainly not the only place where machismo exists, but let's face it: "machismo" is originally a (Mexican) Spanish word. And the concept of the "manly man" has certainly been celebrated—and occasionally mocked—in the language itself. The good news is that most of these expressions can be used by women, too, so now *all* of us can beat our chests and say macho things before setting off to slay dragons or vanquish stout enemies.

La barba me huele a tigre,
   y yo mismo me tengo miedo.

My beard smells of tiger,
   and I'm even afraid of myself.

Steer way clear of anyone who says this.
Heard on the coast of Colombia.

¿Quién dijo miedo,
   si para morir nacimos?

Who said (anything about) fear,
   if we were all born to die?

Imagine yourself riding up and down the line of
troops, inspiring them before the final battle.

**Aquí hasta el más chimuelo masca fierro,
y el más pelón se hace trenzas.**

*Here even the most toothless one chews iron,
and the baldest one does braids.*

How badass is a place where the bald guys do
braids?? This expression is another way of saying
that even the supposed "lesser" of us can be pretty
accomplished (or kick your butt)—so don't underes-
timate them or put them down. Other versions have
the toothless one chewing rails, nuts (the ones that go
with bolts), and stones: *rieles, tuercas, piedras.*

Me hace lo que el viento a Juárez.

It does to me what the wind did to Juárez.

This saying supposedly has its origins not in the
fearless leader himself—Mexican president and
national hero Benito Juárez—but in a statue of him.
Legend has it that a statue of Juárez survived a severe
hurricane unscathed, despite the trees and buildings
around it being demolished. So in Mexico, this is a
way to say you are unflappable and unwilling to bow
to pressure or threats.

Aquí nomás mis chicharrones truenan.

Here, only my pork rinds are crunchy.

You're just going to have to trust me that this sounds
waaaay more macho in Spanish.

**A mí las calacas me pelan los dientes,
   y los perros me bailan la rumba.**

*Skeletons show me their teeth, and dogs dance
   the rumba around me.*

It's amazing just how close tough-sounding and
ridiculous-sounding can seem . . .

**No somos machos,
   pero somos muchos.**

*We're not so tough,
   but there are a lot of us.*

Sometimes numerical advantage outweighs valor,
apparently. Who cares if you're outclassed if you've
got the other side outnumbered?
   Now sometimes heard the other way around,
usually for ironic (or maybe hopeful) effect when
you are outnumbered and you're expecting to get it
handed to you:

No somos muchos, ¡pero somos machos!

El valiente vive hasta que el cobarde quiere.

*The brave one lives only as long as the
    coward wants.*

Bullies can only bully until those being bullied decide
to stand up to them. So when the erstwhile "coward" stands up to the tough guy, that's the end of the
tough guy's run. A tearjerker of a movie was made in
Mexico in 1979 with just this title.

Hierba mala nunca muere.

Bad weeds never die.

Hierba (sometimes *yerba*) *mala* in this case means bad
elements, incorrigible rogues, and scoundrels. Even
if you stand up to them, it sometimes seems that you
just can't get rid of them—like crabgrass.

Can be used when a friend gets sick as a fun way
of saying, "You'll get better soon, I'm sure." Just
make sure it's a close friend—and that they are not
that sick.

**El valiente muere sólo una vez,
el cobarde muere mil veces.**

*A coward dies a thousand deaths,
a brave man only once.*

Okay, I will concede that William Shakespeare was
not technically a Latino. . . . But his line from *Julius
Caesar* about heroes and cowards (popularly, "Cowards die many times before their deaths/ The brave
experience death only once") sure sounds good in
Spanish. The idea here is that a coward dies a little bit
each time he or she is afraid to take a stand, while the
brave die just once—although, let's be fair, probably a
few decades before the coward.

7. *Los penitentes**

More often than you might think, *dichos* and sayings in Spanish are rolled out to put a dent in someone's public image. In other words, they're used as put-downs. Compared to a rude remark or even an obscenity flung in their face, this is a more sophisticated way to take the wind out of someone's sails. Here is a small handful of expressions that can help you diss and dismiss those who distress you.

Ni picha, ni cacha, ni deja batear

Doesn't pitch, catch, or let (others) bat

An expression using baseball lingo—and the anglicized version of it as well—to put down someone who is in the way or just generally useless, like a baseball player who neither pitches, catches, nor lets anyone bat. By extension, it can apply to someone who won't make a decision, like a boss holding up a project for no apparent reason.

Dios los cría, y ellos se juntan.

God creates them, and they get together
(on their own).

When confronted with a group of oddballs, you can
use this expression to dismiss the whole lot with
a mere seven words. The wording itself may suggest a neutral stance—like "birds of a feather flock
together"—but in actual usage, it strongly conveys a
put-down, more like "Jeez Marie, it takes all
kinds . . ."

La memoria es la inteligencia de los pendejos.

Memory is the intelligence of the assholes.

This sharp put-down is reserved for people who quote from memory some impressive fact or statistic. The point: losers like them substitute memorization for intelligence.

Con tierra, agua y tractor,
    cualquier pendejo es agricultor.

With land, water, and a tractor,
    any asshole is an agriculturist.

A sneer at fancy titles—think "sanitation engineer" for janitors or "transparency enhancement facilitator" for window washers.

Es pendejo, pero Dios le ayuda.

He's a stupid fool, but God helps him.

In other words, sometimes it's better to be lucky than good. Perhaps divine intervention explains why certain fools seem to do all right for themselves.

It can be turned around on oneself to say, in effect, "I may be stupid but I'm not *that* stupid," when someone tries to take advantage of you. Fun variants:

Soy tonto, pero no tanto.

I'm a fool, but not that much of one.

Soy tonto, pero nomás de la cabeza.

I'm stupid, but only in the head.

Amor de lejos es de pen . . . sarse (pendejos).

Long-distance love is for . . . thinking
about (losers).

This is the classic line to put down all long-distance relationships. Usually it's enough to use the clean version, with the hesitation on *pen . . . sarse*. People will know what you mean, and may even answer with the even more cynical version:

Amor de lejos, felices los cuatro.

Long-distance love, all four are happy.

**En tierra de ciegos,
	el tuerto es rey.**

*In the land of the blind,
	the one-eyed man is king.*

This wonderful expression actually dates back to
the Dutch scholar Erasmus in the year 1500, give
or take. But it is well enough known in Spanish
that it deserves a place here. It is not technically a
put-down—more of a backhanded compliment. The
"king" in this case might be someone pretty mediocre
who, by being surrounded by incompetents, seems
accomplished. Some have equated it with "a big fish
in a small pond."

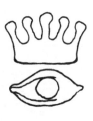

8. Buenos consejos

As we've seen, a main function of proverbs down through the ages has been to encapsulate useful advice for their listeners. A pithy saying can summarize life lessons and set you on the path to a happier, more trouble-free existence. Here are some you may hear south of the border, but that can help you live better on either side of it.

Como te ven te tratan.

How they see you is how they treat you.

This is a useful reminder to those who dress sloppily and don't comb their hair—in other words, most of us while on vacation. On the other hand, if you wear a suit and tie to traffic court, you might just get off with a warning. Appearances matter, at least to the users of this *dicho*.

El buen juez por su casa empieza.

A good judge starts at home.

The meaning here is that before trying to fix the problems of the world (country, city, neighborhood), a person should make sure their own house is in order, that is, start closer to home. There's a clear hint or even accusation of hypocrisy in here. The expression can sometimes be heard when one country scolds another over its human rights record (or environmental practices, or subsidy policies, etc.) when its record at home is less than faultless. It brings to mind folks living in glass houses . . .

Camarón que se duerme se lo lleva la corriente.

The shrimp that sleeps gets carried away by the current.

Clearly, this harkens back to a time when people paid more attention to the sleep habits of crustaceans. But the point is relevant to our daily lives: if you aren't paying attention, you'll get swept away by events. In other words, "You snooze, you lose." Universally used.

Armadillo que se duerme se convierte en charango.

The armadillo that sleeps gets turned into a charango.

A variant, with yet another sleepy animal facing cruel consequences. Here you need to know that a *charango* is an Andean mandolin-like musical instrument—which can be made of armadillo shell. This is a humorous version of the sleeping-shrimp saying.

Más vale solo que mal acompañado.

You're better off alone than in bad company.

Very true. Used as the Spanish title of the 1987 film
Planes, Trains and Automobiles, with Steve Martin
and John Candy.

Cuando el río suena, (es que) agua lleva.

When the river makes noise, it's carrying water.

Much like "where there's smoke, there's fire," and
suggesting that if you hear a rumor, there's likely
some truth to it. The expression makes more sense
in arid country, where rivers might only be audible
after a heavy rainstorm. In some places you may
hear variants, or perhaps the original version, such
as *Cuando el río suena, piedras trae*—"When the river
makes noise, it's carrying rocks"—or even the generic
Cuando el río suena, algo lleva—" . . . it's carrying
something."

A río revuelto, ganancia del pescador (de pescadores).

A turbulent river is a bonanza for the fisherman.

Think about the famous case of the Chinese character for "crisis" combining the characters for "risk" and "opportunity." So a rough river can actually be good for fishing—that is, any tumultuous circumstance can create opportunities for those clever enough to see them. Useful for when the going gets tough, and you want to get going.

Todo cabe en un jarrito, sabiéndolo acomodar.

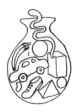

Everything fits in a pitcher if you know how to make it fit.

But then it would, wouldn't it?

Useful when packing the car for the beach vacation and the umbrella just barely sneaks in behind the spare tire ...

Ni tanto que queme al santo, ni tan poco que no lo alumbre

Not so close as to burn the saint, but not so far that it doesn't illuminate it either

To get this expression you have to know that it's referring to holding a candle up to a statue of a saint, as when you light and hold a votive candle in church. The meaning however has nothing to do with religion or saints. Instead it's a way of talking about getting something "just right." This sometimes gets called the Goldilocks principle in English: a porridge that's neither too hot nor too cold, but right in the middle.

La nuez no cae lejos del árbol.

The nut doesn't fall far from the tree.

The "nut" in this case is the child, and the "tree" the parent. So don't be surprised if Junior starts kicking a soccer ball around if Dad was a professional player. Or if Mom was a hothead and the daughter packs a temper, well, whaddya expect? A similar expression, also common, is:

De tal palo, tal astilla

From the same stick, the same splinter

In English, these equate to "Like father, like son," "A chip off the old block," and others.

**En casa del jabonero,
el que no cae resbala.**

*In the soapmaker's house,
he who doesn't fall slips.*

Basically, "We're all in this together," like it or not.
No one can decide *not* to be part of the group when
things start getting sticky—or slippery.

Del árbol caído, todos hacen leña.

From a fallen tree, everyone makes kindling.

As soon as you're down, people start taking
advantage of you, piling on and stepping all over
you—maybe even kicking you while you're down.
In Spanish, it's this tree expression that tells that
sad story. It's all about opportunists and their cruel
behavior.

El que se va a Sevilla pierde su silla.

Those who go to Sevilla lose their seat.

This expression means that if you get up—say to get a beer in the kitchen—I am totally justified in stealing your seat. Finders keepers, more or less.

What's fun about this expression (this is presumably the original version from Spain) is how it adapts so well to each local setting. So in Mexico you will hear *El que se va a la Villa* (i.e., the Basílica of Guadalupe, north of Mexico City); in Colombia, *El que se va a Barranquilla*; in Chile, *El que se va a Melipilla*; and so on. In Ecuador, I'm told, it's *El que se va a Quito pierde su banquito*—his stool. So pull out a map and make up your own!

9. Mejores consejos

As important as it is to soak up the wisdom of the elders, sometimes the didactic route just doesn't cut it. Instead we look for proverbs that are less about stitches and gift horses and more about, well, making you think. So here are some things you will wish you'd been told long ago—mostly so you would have had more time to figure out what exactly they were on about.

Una cosa es una cosa,
   y otra cosa es otra cosa.

One thing is one thing,
   and another thing is another thing.

This is an expression that usually gets pulled out when someone is seen to be taking advantage of us and asking for more than is reasonable. It falls into the "ask for an inch but take a mile" category. So "one thing" might be to ask your mom for a ride to the mall; "another thing" is to ask for the keys to your mom's Mercedes to drive yourself to the mall—when you're only fourteen years old.

Una cosa es Juan Domínguez, y otra cosa es "no me chingues."

One thing is Juan Domínguez, and another thing is "don't screw with me."

A somewhat amped-up and vulgar version of the previous expression, and one you might hear in Mexico. It has the virtue of making a nice rhyme: Juan Domínguez, of course, is only there to rhyme with *chingues*.

If you want to achieve the humorous effect without using the not-for-polite-company "ch-" word, you can always just say the first part of the phrase: *Una cosa es Juan Domínguez. . . .* Then again, just how polite is this company if you have to ask them not to screw with you?

Más vale tarde que nunca

Better late than never

Más vale tarde que más tarde

Better late than later

The first of these is the old stand-by, identical to its English version. The second one is a humorous variant and a little more fun. Also, for when you arrive late but full of energy and rarin' to go:

Tarde pero sin sueño

Late but not tired

Para hacer guisado de liebre se necesita la liebre.

To make hare stew, you need a hare.

In case you were wondering why people say your hare stew sucks.

**Nunca le pegues a un hombre caído,
porque puede levantarse.**

*Never hit a man when he's down,
because he might get up.*

This saying is of course a reworking of the rather tamer injunction about not hitting a man when he's down simply because it's considered unsporting. It is reminiscent of the humorous reworking of the expression "Before you criticize someone, you should walk a mile in their shoes," with the further explanation: "That way when you criticize them, you are a mile away *and* you have their shoes!"

No hay que buscarle tres pies al gato.

Don't search for three legs on a cat.

This is a *dicho* that even scholars have a hard time figuring out. It may even be a deformation of whatever the heck it was originally. (Some say it should be *traspies*, or "stumbles," since cats rarely trip.) But if you can avoid trying to make sense of it, you can use it when you are trying to communicate the idea of "Don't look for something that doesn't exist," or even, "If it ain't broke, don't fix it." A version that is rarer but makes more sense is *Buscarle la quinta pata al gato*, or "Look for the cat's fifth leg." In French, incidentally, you are urged not to look for five legs on a sheep.

10. Ya los pajaritos cantan…

In the land of mañana, it's only natural that some expressions call on their listeners to slow things down a little and take it easy. But it's truly amazing to see the number of expressions that exist urging you to spare your energy. How on earth did anyone find the energy to invent them??

First we will present a selection of finger-wagging expressions telling you to get off your backside and face the day. Then (although thinking about it exhausts us, frankly) we'll give you some retorts to do the exact opposite.

Si quieres dinero y fama,
   que no te agarre el sol en la cama.

If you want riches and fame,
   then don't let the sun catch you in bed.

The first of several expressions that are meant to rouse us at sunrise from a sound sleep and cozy blankets. Of course, this is probably the *worst* possible time for someone to be rambling on about riches and fame. But they don't give up that easily . . .

No hay árbol de tortillas.

Tortillas don't grow on trees.

Sunrise is also a bad time for a botany lesson. Then again, apples, oranges, cashews, and lots of other things *do* grow on trees. Something to ponder as you slowly drift back to sleep.

Al que madruga, Dios lo ayuda.

God helps those who arise early.

In other words, "The early bird gets the worm."
This golden oldie is the mother of all "rise and shine"
proverbs.
    But enough already. The wags have been lying
in bed awhile now, cooking up their counterattack.
Here are two of their versions:

El que madruga . . . encuentra todo cerrado.

Those who rise early . . . find everything closed.

Al que madruga, Dios lo arruga.

Those who rise early God wrinkles.

**No por mucho madrugar
amanece más temprano.**

*Just because you wake up earlier,
dawn doesn't come any sooner.*

An even more elegant way to shush anyone trying to prod you out of bed. What's the rush? Yawn.

**No dejes para mañana lo que puedes hacer
pasado mañana.**

*Don't leave for tomorrow what you can do the
day after tomorrow.*

Another twist on a classic. This one is sometimes attributed to Mark Twain, but one wonders if Twain himself didn't pick it up as an innocent abroad in a Madrid café, sipping a cool sangria. I could check, I suppose, but I think I'll leave it for the day after tomorrow . . .

La ociosidad es la madre de todos los vicios.

Laziness is the mother of all vices.

They just won't go away with their advice! Another dreary classic meant to motivate and energize—to which you can always respond, in good Mexican slang:

**La ociosidad es la madre de . . .
        ¡una vida padre!**

Laziness is the mother of . . . a cool life!

**Si ves a alguien descansando,
        ¡ayúdalo!**

*If you see someone resting,
        help them out!*

I first heard this one from a friend from Tarija, Bolivia, and have ever since dreamed of an extended vacation in Tarija, where people seem to have their priorities straight.

**Nunca nadie ha muerto por
mucho descansar.**

No one has ever died from resting too much.

Probably true, and this one enables you to brush aside
others' advice with solid statistics. Blind them with
science.

**Algo malo debe tener el trabajo, o
los ricos ya lo habrían acaparado.**

*There must be something wrong with work,
or the rich would have kept it for themselves.*

More logical reasoning to dispel the "get a job"
crowd, this one attributed to Cantinflas. If they insist
and say you need to earn money, counter with:

**Si el trabajo diera dinero,
el burro tendría chequera.**

*If work gave you money,
burros would have checkbooks.*

**Que trabajen los casados,
   que tienen obligación.**

*Let married people work; after all,
   they have obligations.*

The logic of these excuses is getting a bit thin, but
keep 'em coming and maybe they will leave you alone.
(Unless you happen to be married, then skip this one.)

**Hay que trabajar para vivir,
   no vivir para trabajar.**

One should work to live, not live to work.

The next time they roll out "work-life balance" on
you, think about this nugget of real wisdom. Get this
one right and a lot of other things just fall into place!
Similarly:

**Tres veces borrico quien vive pobre
   por morir rico**

Three times an ass one who lives poor to die rich

11. *San Lunes*

Despite our best efforts, sometimes it's simply unavoidable to roll out of bed and go to work. A few aphoristic gems have been invented that target Mondays specifically as the day that rest ends for the weary. These bits of wisdom may come in handy as you slump in your desk chair and hug your cup of coffee on a Monday morning around 11:30 a.m.

Los lunes, ni las gallinas ponen.

On Mondays, not even hens lay eggs.

Start the week by lowering expectations. Great start!

**¿Cómo se llama el primo de
Plácido Domingo?**

Maldito (Pinche) Lunes.

What's Placido Domingo's cousin's name?

Damn (Crappy) Monday.

Not a proverb, of course, but a pretty good joke
to begin the week. To get it, it helps to know that
"Plácido Domingo," besides being the name of a
world-famous opera singer, translates as "Placid
Sunday."

Mal comienza la semana para quien ahorcan el lunes.

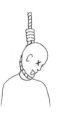

The week starts poorly for one who gets hanged on Monday.

Another one of those marvelous Captain Obvious proverbs with information we could scarcely have figured out for ourselves—which makes them all the more amusing. This *dicho* can refer to any situation that gets off to a horrible start—if your team takes two goals in the first ten minutes, for instance. Or in expectation, if Monday morning your boss calls you into her office, and you prepare for the worst.

Hizo su San Lunes.

He's taking St. Monday off.

One age-old technique to avoid the trauma of a Monday morning is simply to take it off, dressing it up as a feast day: St. Monday.

While invoking San Lunes is an effective short-term strategy, it's the rare boss who doesn't catch on pretty quickly—which may explain why you never hear about St. Tuesday . . .

12. *De vuelta al yugo**

* *Yugo* is "yoke," that is, "back to the salt mines."

Arguably the worst thing about a Monday is that it is followed by four more days of work. And yet the work week and workplace make for very fertile soil for *dichos*. After all, what else are you going to do during office hours but think up pithy things to say?

Some of these *dichos* exalt the dignity of work, others curse it (see the previous sections), and still others blame the terrible creature—the boss—who keeps your nose pressed to the grindstone. Here are a few—to read in your free time, of course.

Cualquiera toca el cilindro,
pero no cualquiera lo carga.

*Anyone can play a street organ,
but not everyone can carry it.*

On the streets of Latin America you will sometimes come across an old-style organ-grinder (the traditional monkey is less common these days). The organs are bulky, heavy, Austrian-made windup organs, which they play while passing the hat for donations. Playing it is easy, says the *dicho*, but carrying it is worth some spare change. By extension, it applies to any job that looks easy but isn't.

En las horas de trabajo,
¡los amigos al carajo!

During work hours, to hell with friends!

This is the sort of thing a red-faced bellowing boss might tell you when he catches you making a personal call or receiving friends when you're "on the clock." You can use it yourself with your friends, but they probably won't continue to be your friends for very long.

El flojo trabaja doble.

The lazy man works double.

Taking lazy shortcuts on a task will end up costing you more work down the road, or so this *dicho* would have us believe. So if in taking out the trash you don't seal the lids tightly, and the neighborhood dogs get in and spread the trash around, you will now have to clean that up as well—and work double. Likewise, if you do a sloppy job on a report, and your boss tells you to do it all over again. Of course, a true *flojo* wouldn't work at all, but that's not what they want you to conclude here.

**El que manda, manda,
     y si se equivoca, vuelve a mandar.**

*He who calls the shots, calls the shots, and if he
     makes a mistake, he'll call the shots again.*

Some bosses seem to have special protection (or a
family connection) that keeps them around no matter
what they do or how poorly they do it. It ain't fair, but
it's the way it is. This expression, whispered out of
the boss's earshot, is one small way to even the score.

El que sabe, sabe, y el que no (sabe) es gerente.

*He who knows, knows, and he who doesn't (know)
     is the manager.*

More abuse for bosses who don't seem to understand
how things get done on the job—but are the bosses
anyway.

   This is a waggish variant on George Bernard
Shaw's also waggish original: "He who can, does; he
who cannot, teaches."

**Estando bien con Dios,
los santos salen sobrando.**

*When you're in good with God,
who needs saints?*

If you can't lick 'em, you can always suck up to those nasty bosses. This *dicho* reminds us that if you can get in good with the Big Boss, you can pretty much ignore everyone else around the workplace. Likewise,

**¿Por qué hablar con el payaso si puedes
hablar con el dueño del circo?**

*Why talk with the clown if you can talk with the
owner of the circus?*

Hay que estar cerca del que paga y lejos del que manda.

It's best to be close to the paymaster and far from the one in charge.

Here is another wise workplace survival strategy— although the opposite in a way of the previous one. Here you want to fly under the boss's radar, and then collect your paycheck and slink quietly home.

Se cree la mamá de Tarzán.

She (or he) thinks herself (or himself) the mother of Tarzan.

No one seems to know why Tarzan's mom was selected for this *dicho*, but for some reason she has been made the epitome of the coworker who acts like he or she is the boss or has some special authority— but really isn't and doesn't. In English, a good way of conveying this is the sneer "So who died and made *you* boss?"

These same folks might also think themselves *la última Pepsi del desierto, la última chupada del mango,* or *la última chela del estadio* ("the last Pepsi in the desert," "the last suck of a mango," or "the last beer in the stadium").

13. *Los clásicos*

Proverbs go back ages, to a time when people gave horses as gifts and whatnot. So it's not surprising that these tidbits of folk wisdom have over the centuries crossed from language to language, giving us *dichos* that are virtually the same in Spanish and in English. In other cases, the wisdom survives, but the expression varies. Here is a quick list.

**A caballo regalado,
no se le mira el diente.**

*Never look a gift horse in the
tooth (mouth).*

El fin justifica los medios.

The end justifies the means.

Quien ríe al último ríe mejor.

The one who laughs last laughs best.

**Más vale malo por conocido que bueno
por conocer.**

*Better the bad one you know than the good one
you don't. (Better the devil you know than
the devil you don't.)*

Con este amigo, ¿para qué quiero enemigos?

With friends like that, who needs enemies?

Es pan comido.

It's eaten bread (a piece of cake).

No se sufre por lo que no se sabe.

What you don't know won't hurt you.

Al que le quede el saco, que se lo ponga.

If the suit coat (shoe) fits, wear it.

El que madruga coge la oruga.

The early bird gets the worm.

Roma no se construyó en un día.

Rome wasn't built in a day.

¿De qué sirve llorar sobre la leche derramada?

Why bother crying over spilled milk?

**El que a hierro mata, a hierro muere
(termina).**

*Those who kill by iron, die by iron.
    (Live by the sword, die by the sword.)*

**Cuando sale el gato,
    los ratones hacen fiesta.**

*When the cat's away, the mice have
    a party (will play).*

Más vale pájaro en mano que cien volando

*Better a bird in the hand than one hundred flying
    (two in the bush)*

Now for some with similar messages but in different wrappings:

Ahogado el niño, tapan el pozo.

Cover the well after the child has drowned. (Close the barn door after the cows have escaped.)

Hoy por mí, mañana por ti.

Today for me, tomorrow for you. (You scratch my back, I'll scratch yours.)

A donde fueres, haz lo que vieres.

Wherever you go, do what you see. (When in Rome, do as the Romans do.)

**Cuando está más oscuro,
brillan las estrellas.**

*The stars are brightest when it is
darkest. (It's always darkest
just before the dawn.)*

**La gota que
derramó/rebalsó el vaso.**

*The drop that made the cup
spill over. (The straw that
broke the camel's back.)*

**Ojos que no ven,
corazón que no siente.**

*Eyes that don't see, heart that
doesn't feel. (Out of sight, out of mind.)*

A buen entendedor, pocas palabras.

To one who understands well, few words.
(A word to the wise.)

Es como llevar leña al monte.

It's like taking firewood to the forest.
(. . . coals to Newcastle.)

Dejar la iglesia en manos de Lutero.

Leaving the church in the hands of Luther (foxes
to guard the henhouse). Note that some
Lutherans (and others) may take offense at
this somewhat scurrilous expression from
the Counter-Reformation.

El que no llora no mama.

He who doesn't cry doesn't suckle. (The squeaky
wheel gets the grease.)

**Les das la mano,
    y te agarran el pie.**

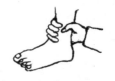

*You give them a hand, and they grab your foot.
    (Give them an inch, and they'll take a mile.)*

Pedirle peras al olmo.

*Ask for pears from the elm tree. (Bark up the
    wrong tree.)*

Querer es poder.

*Wanting to is being able to.
    (Where there's a will there's a way.)*

No tengo vela en este entierro.

*I don't have a candle at this burial.
    (I don't have a dog in this fight.)*

14. Es un buen tipo...

Getting on in years is a part of life. It has its drawbacks, of course, but all things considered, it's better than the alternative. And as time passes and we pass through this vale of tears, the *dichos* keep up with us, shedding light on the vicissitudes of our existence and maybe poking a little fun at ourselves as we go.

Sabe más el diablo por viejo que por diablo.

The devil knows more from being old than from being the devil.

A way of acknowledging someone who has been around for a long time and picked up some wisdom—"knows where the bodies are buried," as it were. It's something of a backhanded compliment, as it may imply that the person doesn't know a lot because of their exceptional intelligence so much as because of their longevity. But at heart it's a begrudging recognition of an old-timer's years of experience.

Si necesitas consejo, pídelo al viejo.

If you need advice, ask the old guy.

Another *dicho* confirming that at least some *dichos*
are invented by old people who would like to think
that the world thinks this way.

There is, of course, a different version that was
probably invented by someone considerably younger:

Entre más viejo, más pendejo

The older, the stupider

**No pienses que soy viejo;
lo que soy es mal cuidado.**

*Don't think of me as old;
I'm just poorly maintained.*

Or perhaps: "It ain't the age, it's the mileage," which
can also be heard in Spanish as *No es la edad, sino
el kilometraje*—courtesy originally of Indiana Jones,
whose version was "It's not the years, it's the mileage."

**Si después de los cincuenta nada te duele,
es que estás muerto.**

If after you turn fifty nothing hurts, you're dead.

A little something to look forward to.

Se quedó para vestir santos.

She stayed to dress saints.

The concept of "old maid," while not politically correct, is prevalent in many societies. This *dicho* traditionally describes a woman—although presumably it could be a man as well—who didn't get married and instead spends time dressing the saints for religious ceremonies.

There is a nice retort, however:

**¡Es mejor vestir santos que
desvestir borrachos!**

*It's better to dress saints than to
undress drunkards!*

**De los cuarenta para arriba,
no te mojes la barriga.**

From forty on, don't wet your belly.

I really have no idea what this one is supposed to
mean—apparently it's a warning to "old folks"—those
who have rounded year forty and are in imminent and
irreversible decline—not to expose themselves to chills
and such when they are so decrepit and fragile. Plus it
doesn't even really rhyme. But it is such a goofy expression, I felt compelled to include it here. I hope that
somewhere, someone over forty has founded a Belly-
wetters Club of people having the time of their lives.

**En todas las casas debe haber un viejo y un
burro, pero que ni el viejo sea tan burro
ni el burro tan viejo.**

*In every home there should be an old person and
a burro, but the old person shouldn't be too
burro (stupid) nor the burro too old.*

Self-explanatory, although it's rare to find a house
anymore that keeps an old person and a burro around.
Shame.

15. *Colgando los tenis*[*]

---

[*] Useful tidbit: In Mexican slang, *colgar los tenis*, or "hang up your sneakers," means "to die." Some even conjecture that it is tied to the custom of hanging shoes from power lines, said to indicate that someone has died.

Death is a part of life, too. The very, very last part, to be more specific. And as such it has a way of focusing the mind. And once a mind starts to focus, can a *dicho* be far behind? Of course not, which is why the Grim Reaper gets a large share of *dichos* dedicated to him and by extension to that all-too-brief period that comes just before his visit: our life.

De nada sirve ser el más rico del panteón.

There's no point being the richest person in the cemetery.

In short, you can't take it with you. But if you decide to, you will be the richest person in the cemetery!

Cuando el tecolote canta, el indio muere; no es cierto, pero sucede.

When the owl sings, the Indian dies; it isn't true, but it happens.

In many traditional cultures, owls are associated with death, and from that belief in Aztec Mexico comes this *dicho*. The best part, however, is the tag-on ending, which is as pure a statement of folk thinking as exists—recognizing the absurdity of blaming the owl, but at the same time stating that it really happens that way nonetheless. An early version of cognitive dissonance or even fake news??

**Lo malo de la inmortalidad
es que hay que morir
para alcanzarla.**

*The problem with immortality
is you have to die to achieve it.*

To add to the mystery, the younger you die—rock
singers and movie stars, for instance—the *more*
immortal you become. Spooky.

¿Quieres saber tus virtudes? ¡Muérete!

Want to hear about your virtues? Die!

If we'd only tell each other how great we are when
we're alive, what a wonderful world it would be. But
then what fun would funerals be?

**Al que se aleja lo olvidan,
    y al que se muere lo entierran.**

*He who goes away is forgotten,
    and he who dies is buried.*

A pretty sad and cynical lens to view life through.
"Out of sight, out of mind" is often given as a translation. But it calls to mind even gloomier maxims, such
as "The graveyards are full of indispensable people."

El muerto al pozo y el vivo al gozo

*The dead into the well and the living to have fun
    (raise hell?)*

Now that's more like it! Liven up your next funeral
with this exclamation!

In common usage, you might hear "Let the dead
bury their dead" to convey this apparent disregard
for the deceased, but that expression (from the Bible)
doesn't really mean that. "Life goes on" is probably
the closest to the sentiment here.

**¿Quién se quiere morir con lo caras
que están las flores?**

*Who wants to die with flowers costing
what they do?*

Now this is the right way to look at life's ending: as a
nuisance and an unnecessary expense!

16. Inventando pretextos

Proverbs seem unusually well suited to calling someone's bluff or shining a light on how lame their excuses are, probably because it's rude to come right out and say "Bullshit!," whereas a good *dicho* allows you to softly and gently stick the dagger in.

Si mi abuela tuviera ruedas, sería bicicleta.

*If my grandmother had wheels, she would be
a bicycle.*

One of a lengthy list of expressions that serve to
dismiss unceremoniously another person's claim
that things would be different "If only . . ." A quaint
equivalent in English is "If ifs and buts were candy
and nuts, we'd all have a merry Christmas." Or if you
prefer a ruder and more wicked version: "If mud had
a square rear, would it shit square bricks?"

Here are a couple of other variants:

Si mi tía tuviera barba/cojones, sería mi tío.

*If my aunt had a beard/balls, she would
be my uncle.*

**Si las barbas valieran,
los chivos serían generales.**

*If beards were worth something,
goats would be generals.*

**Si los deseos fueran caballos,
   los mendigos serían jinetes.**

If wishes were horses, beggars would ride.

This one, originally an English proverb, has now
become well known in Spanish.

**Si el mar fuera vino,
   todo el mundo sería marino.**

If the sea were wine, we'd all be sailors.

First heard in Chile, which is well endowed with both
sea and wine.

Se me olvidó que el alcohol emborrachaba.

I forgot that alcohol makes you drunk.

Oh sure, never mind, then.

Si se curó, fue la Virgen; si se murió, fue el doctor.

*If (the patient) gets well, it was the Virgin Mary; if
the patient dies, it was the doctor.*

Reminiscent of the expression "Victory has a hundred
fathers, but defeat is an orphan." Here the poor doctor
gets only blame, never the credit.

Poner la cara de "yo no fui"

Put on the face of "it wasn't me"

This face of feigned innocence is most often associated
with kids—especially ones who break a vase or traipse
mud onto the carpet. However, grown-ups have been
known to use it as well (Ha! Look at yourself in the mirror!).

Another version is:

Hacerse la mosquita muerta

Make like a dead fly

Dead flies can't knock over vases, after all.

Desde que se inventaron las excusas, se acabaron los pretextos.

Ever since they invented excuses, there were no more pretexts.

This deliberately senseless expression for dismissing excuses has since been almost completely replaced in common usage by the classic, incisive:

Desde que se inventaron los pretextos, se acabaron los idiotas/pendejos.

Ever since they invented excuses, there were no more idiots/shitheads.

Usually, it's enough just to shake your head and say the first part: *Sí, claro, desde que se inventaron los pretextos . . .*

17. *El reino animal*

The animal world is an endless source of raw material for *dichos*. Humans' faithful companions down through the ages, cats and dogs especially, appear a lot in our wordplay and folk wisdom.

De noche, todos los gatos son pardos.

At night, all cats are brown.

The more common English version of this expression uses "gray" instead of "brown," but the meaning is the same: In the dark, things tend to look all the same, and a person's beauty—or lack thereof—tends to be hidden. By extension, so too can a person's intentions seem obscure in the dark of night.

Si te digo que la burra es parda, es porque tengo los pelos en la mano.

If I tell you the burro is brown, it's because I've got its hairs in my hand.

Continuing with the brown animal theme, this *dicho* is saying with some vigor, "Trust me on this one, I got proof." And why not? A person who will yank out a donkey's hair to prove the hair color is probably a good bet to be detail oriented and get the facts right.

El que no tiene perro, con su gato va al monte.

He who doesn't have a dog, takes his cat into the woods (e.g., hunting).

A cat, as you can imagine, is a lousy companion for a hike in the woods (unless *you* want to follow *it*). But you have to make do with what you got, this *dicho* tells us.

Gato escaldado tiene miedo del agua fría.

A scalded cat is afraid of cold water.

It's somewhat amazing how often this phrase comes in handy. It is reminiscent of "Once bitten, twice shy," or even, "Fooled once, shame on you; fooled twice, shame on me." But the twist is making the water cold, meaning that even if the second time around the threat isn't so bad, the victim will take no chances and assume it is.

Muerto el perro,
se acabó la rabia.

Once the dog is dead,
the rabies ends.

In other words, go to the source to stop something; it's the only way to make sure the problem goes away for good.

(*Notice:* No dogs were harmed in the making of this book.)

Aquí hay gato encerrado.

There's an enclosed cat here.

The literal translation doesn't get you close to this *dicho*'s gruesome truth. If you think of a cat being locked in or enclosed somewhere and not being able to get out, and then you think of that same cat about a week or a month later, you start to get the picture. "Something is rotten in the state of Denmark" or "Something's fishy" conveys the same odorous concern. Or even just "Something here just doesn't smell right." It's used to express suspicions that things may not be on the up-and-up.

Perro que ladra no muerde.

A barking dog doesn't bite.

This one sounds wise, but who wants to be the first to test it? Used most often in the figurative sense, it suggests that the loud blowhard or trash-talker is probably all bluff. A similar sentiment exists in the English expression "Its bark is worse than its bite."

Si quieres el perro, acepta las pulgas.

If you want the dog, accept the fleas.

A.k.a. "Every rose has its thorn," and no one is perfect. This works as advice to anyone complaining about their mate.

**Me extraña, araña, que siendo mosca
    no me conozcas.**

*It surprises me, spider, that being a fly you
    don't know me.*

**Me extraña que siendo araña (. . . te caigas de
    la pared).**

*It surprises me that being a spider (. . . you fall off
    the wall).*

Two good spider expressions (you can never get
enough of those). The first one plays with internal
rhyme to say to someone who knows you well, basically, "Have you *met* me?" The second is said to
someone who claims to have it figured out . . . then
bombs. "Man, I thought you *had* this . . ."

Los pájaros disparándoles a las escopetas

Birds shooting at shotguns

This is a fine phrase to describe things that seem to be, well, bass-ackward. It fits nicely for cases of family or workplace rebellion or insubordination—the employees telling the boss she has to work Saturday, or Junior telling Dad he has to be back by eleven, and with gas in the tank. "Hey, whaddya know? The rebels destroyed the Death Star!" "Really? *¡Los pájaros disparándoles a las escopetas!*"

18. *Símiles y similares*

Some of the most colorful creations in any language are in the realm of comparisons: one thing as it stacks up against another. The juxtaposition of unexpected objects can make for incisive, memorable, and amusing descriptions, as this short list of examples shows.

Más nervioso que gato en canoa

More nervous than a cat in a canoe

**Más contento que MacGyver en Homecenter/
Home Depot**

*Happier than MacGyver in
Homecenter/Home Depot*

(Choose the giant hardware store nearest you.)

Más feo que pegarle a Dios en Viernes Santo

Uglier than smacking God on Good Friday

Más flojo que un hippie en una foto

Lazier than a hippie in a photo

(That is, not much movement ...)

Más perdido que Adán en (el) Día de la Madre

More lost/confused than Adam on Mother's Day

Más caro que tener un hijo idiota en Harvard

*More expensive than having an idiot son
at Harvard*

Más falso que moneda de cuero

More fake than a leather coin

Más largo que un día sin pan

Longer than a day without bread

Más largo que un fin de semana sin dinero

Longer than a weekend without money

Más papista que el Papa

More papist than the pope

(This one is used figuratively for someone who is more worked up about something than the people who are actually affected by it.)

Tan claro como el lodo

As clear as mud

Más flaco que silbido de culebra

Thinner than a snake's hiss

Mejor se daña

(Any) better would hurt

"So how are things?" ¡*Mejor se daña!*
("Couldn't be better!")

19. *De boca en boca*

"Discretion is the better part of valor," the proverb tells us. "Better to keep your mouth shut and be thought a fool, than to open it and remove all doubt."

Likewise in Spanish, admonitions from the *dicho* makers encourage us to think about our mouths and, when in doubt, to keep them hermetically sealed.

El pez por la boca muere.

The fish dies by its mouth.

The implication being: And so might you if you don't learn to keep your trap shut. "Loose lips sink ships," after all.

A similar message, this time using flies:

En boca cerrada no entran moscas.

In a closed mouth, flies don't get in.

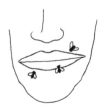

El que calla otorga.

Those who keep silent consent.

If you don't like something, speak up. And if
you don't speak up, don't complain about it later.
This expression applies nicely to voters, or rather
nonvoters, as well.

    Taken to the next level:

Quien calla y obedece se jode dos veces.

One who keeps silent and obeys is
*   doubly screwed.*

A palabras necias, oídos sordos

To stubborn words, deaf ears

A palabras de borracho, oídos de cantinero

To words of a drunk, ears of a bartender

These two expressions are the linguistic equivalent of covering your ears and saying, "Na na na na na na."

El sordo no oye, pero bien que compone.

The deaf one doesn't hear but sure composes well.

Probably an allusion originally to Beethoven, who composed amazing symphonies even after going deaf. If they use this on you, however, they are not comparing you to Beethoven. They are saying you weren't paying attention and have now joined the conversation late with some stupid and presumably invented, or "composed," remark.

Habla más que un perdido cuando lo encuentran.

She talks more than a lost person when found.

"Oh, thank God you found me, I can't believe you're here, you'll never believe what happened, I was …"
First heard in Colombia.

Hablar a calzón quitado

Speak with the underwear off

As strange as it may seem at first, this expression means to speak freely—without reservations or inhibitions. Similar to "bare your soul," although here you are baring something quite different. This is a very widespread expression and can be used in business settings ("Let's talk turkey") or in relationships ("Let's get everything on the table"). And it almost always brings a grin.

No tiene pelos en la lengua.

He has no hair on his tongue.

This is a very common and useful way of describing the sort of person who has no filter at all between brain and tongue. They "speak their mind," in other words, with little regard for others' feelings or diplomatic niceties. It can sometimes refer to someone who laces their speech with obscenities or "talks trash."

"How did you guys like the movie?" "It was okay…" "No it wasn't, it sucked." "*Ay, chico, no tienes pelos en la lengua.*"

20. El podero$o caballero

If there's one area where we are always likely to get someone's advice, it's money and how we should spend it. Many *dichos* have been enlisted to this end, much as they have in English, where a certain fool and his money had a predictable proverbial ending.

Con dinero baila el perro.

For money, the dog will dance.

Okay, maybe it won't. But you can get pretty much anything else you want, and who cares if the dog dances?

A César lo que es de César, y a Dios . . .
¡Que les vaya bien!

To Caesar that which is Caesar's, and to God . . .
Bye! May it go well for them!

A clever reformulation of the biblical advice to pay your taxes to the Romans. The joke hinges on "a Dios," which in addition to being "to God" can be read as *adiós*, as in "see ya later." So you give your local César your hard-earned money, and you can pretty much kiss it good-bye.

Debo, no niego; pago, no tengo.

I owe, I don't deny; but payment I don't have.

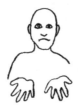

El que nada debe nada teme.

He who owes nothing fears nothing.

Two classic "debt" *dichos*. The first is straightforward and refers most often to plain old monetary debt. The second is more likely to be used figuratively, as in owing favors. If you owe no favors and are in no one's debt, it's that much easier to be fearless.

Dios mío, quítame lo pobre,
      que lo feo se me quita
      con dinero.

Dear God, please make me stop
      being poor; my being ugly
      will go away with money.

You can interpret this how you want, but the basic message is that someone with a lot of money is never really all *that* ugly—or they can invest in the cosmetic treatments needed to change or hide their ugliness. Also:

Dios mío, quítame lo pobre,
      pero no me quites lo huevón.

Dear God, please make me stop being poor, but
      don't stop me from being a lazy bum!

Le salió más caro el caldo que las albóndigas.

*The broth ended up costing more than
    the meatballs.*

Quite a common expression for when the part you
thought would be cheap (the broth) ended up costing
you a lot more than the apparently expensive part
(the meatballs). If, for instance, you take the bus to
save on gas, and the bus breaks down and leaves you
stranded, and you have to spend five times the cost
of the gas on taxis, then your cheaper alternative
will end up costing you more than the "meatballs." It
works for most any situation or solution that back-
fires on you.

El que compra barato, compra a cada rato.

Those who buy cheap, buy often.

Pretty much the definition of a "false economy." You think you're getting a great deal until it breaks, and you have to buy it again.

   Simpler still (but without the rhyme):

Lo barato sale caro.

What's cheap ends up costing you.

El que fía no está.

The guy who lets you buy on credit isn't here.

The sort of sign you can expect to find in a corner store or local bar—right next to the "Free beer tomorrow" sign.

Cuentas claras, amistades largas

Clear accounts, lasting friendships

Las cuentas claras y el chocolate espeso

The accounts clear and the hot chocolate thick

These two versions of the same idea are very
common and very handy when you are delicately
searching for a polite way to insist on clear contract
terms or an IOU from a friend who borrows money
(power tools, etc.).

A glass of thick hot chocolate is anything but clear,
of course.

21. Las penas

Dichos offer us wisdom, of course, but at times they offer us something even more precious: comfort in hard times.

These *dichos* are about suffering from, dealing with, complaining about, and overcoming troubles. If that sounds pretty depressing, rest assured: No good *dicho* devotee would let pass the chance to spit in the face of his or her troubles with a little hard-edged humor.

Me vistieron de cristiano y me aventaron a los leones.

The dressed me as a Christian and threw me to the lions.

Have you ever been told to give a presentation on short notice to your firm's hardest-to-please clients? This is the expression you were looking for to describe that feeling.

"Thrown to the wolves" is the equivalent in English, with the added aggravation of, say, "They dressed me as a sheep . . ." preceding it.

La Ley de Herodes: o te chingas o te jodes.

It's Herod's Law: either you're fucked or
    you're screwed.

One suspects that King Herod never really had a law like this. "Damned if you do, damned if you don't" comes immediately to mind. Or "You can't win for losing."

In the rhyming with "you're screwed" *dicho* category, we also have:

**Se acabó la sopa de fideos;
nomás queda la de jodeos.**

*The noodle soup has run out;
now there's just the you're-screwed soup.*

**Sólo borracho y dormido se me olvida que
estoy jodido.**

*Only drunk and asleep do I forget that
I'm screwed.*

There sure are a lot of ways to rhyme that word and
its variations, which means there are many clever
ways to share your grief—in verse!

Ya no quiero queso,
sino salir de la ratonera.

I don't want any more cheese,
I just want to get out of
the mousetrap.

This *dicho* falls in the Stop-the-World-I-Want-to-Get-Off category, where "cheese" is a reward for continuing to slog on in misery toward some goal.

In a similar vein:

El trabajo no es entrar,
sino encontrar la salida.

The hard part isn't getting in,
but finding a way out.

Some troubles are better off stopped before you begin.

No llames más fantasmas que los que puedas hacer desaparecer.

Don't call more ghosts than you can make disappear.

As a general rule, when calling ghosts, it's best not to overdo it. Think of Harry Potter and the Dementors if you don't believe me. This is not a frequently heard *dicho*, and it's hard to think of a good example of when you would use it—maybe when in an argument with your partner you start to dredge up old affronts?—but it's a cool and ominous-sounding expression nonetheless.

No es lo duro, sino lo tupido.

It's not how hard (they hit) but how often.

This is a common lament for when problems just keep on coming one after the other. The *dicho* suggests that no one blow is all that bad in itself, but that all of them together are hard to handle—a little like battling zombies in a video game. "*Tupido*" means "all bunched together," and its main use in Spanish today is probably in this expression.

Para que sepas lo que es amar a Dios en tierra de infieles

Just so you know what it is to love God in the land of the infidels

Supposedly an expression that got its birth during Spain's colonial era (the other common version is ... *en tierra de indios*), this essentially says, "Now you know what it's like to be all alone and in a bad spot." Parents may use the phrase on their kids, as if to say, "Life's tough, you better get used to it." But for humorous and dramatic effect, you can use it for any rough situation. Walking out of the conference room after that last-minute client presentation a few pages earlier, you might murmur, *"Ahora sé lo que es ..."*

Me traen como perro de rancho: cuando hay bronca, me sueltan, y cuando hay fiesta, me amarran.

They treat me like a ranch dog: when there's trouble, they let me loose, and when there's a party, they tie me up.

It's a dog's life on the ranch, clearly.

Salir de Guatemala para entrar en Guatepeor

Leave Guatemala to enter Guatepeor

The straight translation doesn't help much, of course. What you need to notice is that "*mala*" is "bad" and "*peor*" is "worse." Get it?

An easy English equivalent is "Jump from the frying pan into the fire." It's for use when you finally think you are escaping from a bad stretch of luck—and then it gets even worse.

Éramos pocos, y parió la abuela.

*There were so few of us, and now
Grandma's given birth.*

A fun Spanish proverb used to describe a situation
that you didn't think could get any worse, but does.
Note that "few of us" is meant ironically—in fact,
sometimes you'll hear this dicho as *Éramos muchos*.
The phrase is often used when there's not enough to
go around, and more people suddenly show up. But
it can be applied generically to situations that go
wrong unexpectedly, blindsiding you. His team down
2–1, (Lionel) Messi misses a penalty: *Ay, Dios, ¡éramos
pocos, y parió la abuela!*

La situación está tan mala que si mi mujer se
va con otro, yo me voy con ellos.

*The situation is so bad that if my wife leaves me
for another guy, I'm going with them.*

This may be about as bad as it gets.

**Estando en la mala,
 uno pisa mierda y se resbala.**

*Being in a bad spot,
 one steps in shit and slips.*

A considerably more graphic way of saying, "When it rains, it pours," or maybe, "If it weren't for bad luck, I'd have no luck at all." Lynyrd Skynyrd may have phrased it: "Jump in a rosebush, and come out smelling like shit."

**Las penas no matan,
 pero ayudan a morir.**

*Sorrows won't kill you,
 but they help you die.*

This gets my vote for the saddest *dicho* in the entire book.

Cuidado, que el diablo es puerco.

Careful, the devil is dirty.

This is a common expression in Colombia, where it reportedly got its start in a soap opera where the dad would warn his daughter to be careful around boys. It still has a strong connotation of warning against temptations of the flesh, but you can also hear it to mean more generally: "Watch out, things can go very bad." Basically, it's saying the devil is a mean son-of-a-bitch, so stay on your toes—and be careful out there! Often heard nowadays as simply, *El diablo es puerco.*

Si tiene remedio, ¿por qué te quejas? Si no tiene remedio, ¿por qué te quejas?

If there's a remedy, why complain? If there's no remedy, why complain?

With so many ways of saying how screwed you are, it's only fair that there would be a few responses, ranging from condolence to advice to quit your bellyaching. This *dicho* is an example of the latter. It is variously attributed to an Arab proverb or a Bengali sage.

Hay muertos que no hacen ruido y es más grande su penar.

There are dead people who don't make noise and whose suffering is greater.

In other words, greater than yours. So again, quit your bellyaching. You don't have it all that bad.

Las penas con pan son buenas.

Sorrows with bread are good.

In other words, if you still have food, your troubles aren't *that* bad.

Ahogarse en un vaso de agua

Drown in a glass of water

Again, stop making such a fuss about it.
A.k.a. "Don't make a mountain out of a molehill."
You may hear this if you are worrying frenetically about something that no one else seems to think is a big deal: *¡Hombre, no te ahogues en un vaso de agua!*
Or maybe, if you are losing your head while everyone about you is keeping theirs . . . you may just be drowning in a glass of water.

John Prine fans may recall, "It's a half an inch of water and you think you're going to drown."

Al mal paso darle prisa.

Take bad steps quickly.

This is an old-timer but still quite often heard. The suggestion is to get something unpleasant over with quickly—rip off the band-aid, as it were. It is reminiscent of the great phrase attributed to Churchill: "If you're going through hell, keep going!"

No hay mal que dure 100 años (ni cuerpo/ pendejo que lo aguante).

Nothing bad lasts one hundred years (nor is there a body/S.O.B. who could put up with it).

No hay mal que por bien no venga.

*There is no bad that some good doesn't
come from it.*

These phrases of consolation offer some assurance
that your troubles won't last forever and are worth
the sacrifice. The second one even promises that
elusive "silver lining."

**Cuando no hay remedio pa' las chinches,
hay que quemar el petate.**

*When there's no remedy for the bedbugs,
you've got to burn the bedroll.*

From rural Mexico. When nothing else works and
you're down to your last Pokémon, as it were, you
sometimes just have to start all over and burn the
frickin' bedroll!

22. ¡Ándale, ándale!*

* Attributed to a certain S. González.

You wouldn't think that when you're in a hurry would be a good time to dip into the *dicho* chest, but you'd be wrong. Often a clever phrase is just what is needed to call people's attention and get them to shake a leg, get the lead out, and get the show on the road.

Pa' luego es tarde.

Later is too late.

The time to act is now! A somewhat "country" (rural) expression, but nice and emphatic.

Atáscate ahora que hay lodo.

Get stuck now while there's mud.

A classic. It is often used to suggest "Let's dig in" when food is available, or "Get 'em while they're hot!" But it can apply to any situation where opportunity presents itself, for when better to get stuck than when there's plenty of mud?

   "I was thinking of asking the professor a question, but she's been surrounded by students."

   "Well she's alone now. ¡*Atáscate ahora que hay lodo!*"

Vámonos muriendo todos, que están enterrando gratis.

Let's all get to dying, 'cause they're burying for free.

Another clever *dicho* that is less about dying and more about fleeing from a deathly dull situation. A.k.a. "Let's make like a bakery truck and haul buns," "Let's blow this popsicle stand," "Let's make like Tom and Cruise," and on and on.

Vísteme despacio, que tengo prisa.

Dress me slowly, as I'm in a hurry.

Attributed variously to Don Quixote, Napoleon, and a handful of Spanish kings (this explains why someone would be dressing them), the message is don't hurry up to screw up—that is, "Haste makes waste."

A trimmed-down version is:

¡Date prisa lentamente!

Hurry up slowly!

¿Para qué tanto brinco estando el suelo tan parejo?

Why so much jumping around when the floor is so flat?

A fine, anti-urgency *dicho* that urges calmness. Sometimes invoked by a couple when they find themselves arguing about miniscule stuff. "Don't sweat the small stuff" comes to mind. Or maybe, per Avril Lavigne, "Why do you have to go and make things so complica-a-ted?"

Ahorita

Little "now"

This is an expression in a single word. The meaning varies somewhat by culture (or simply has no meaning, as in Spain), and its official definition is usually given as "right now," but it almost universally it means "*not* now." This could be in the sense of "Gimme a sec, I'm finishing something." Or it could be much less imminent: "When are you going to clean up your room?" *Ahorita* . . . , in other words, "Don't hold your breath." Of course, the person asking might respond, *¡Ahorita es ahorita!* Or "Now means now!" Perhaps, but "*ahorita*" doesn't.

23. *Las redes sociales*

We are social beings, and social settings are some of the best ones to show off your familiarity with a handful of tongue-in-cheek *dichos* designed for just such venues. Whether you're showing up uninvited or overstaying your welcome, you can rely on your trusty *dichos* to say with a swagger what you would probably be too polite to say directly.

Más vale llegar a tiempo que ser invitado

Better to arrive at the right time than to be invited

This is a fun comment to toss out when you've accidentally (yeah, sure) arrived at someone's house right at lunch or dinnertime.

Donde come uno, comen dos (... pero cuesta el doble).

Where one eats, two can eat (... but it costs twice as much).

The original and very common expression says that wherever there is food for n, there is food for $n+1$. In other words, one more mouth to feed is not a big deal. (In Brazil, you might hear *Bota água no feijão*, or "Add some water to the beans," to handle unexpected dinner guests.)

The part in parenthesis above is a sly modern add-on that mischievously undercuts the generosity of the original saying.

Todo lo que camina, repta o vuela—¡a la cazuela!

Anything that walks, crawls, or flies—into the pot!

Another rhymer, this is what you can say when told that the afternoon meal contains rabbit, iguana, and sparrow. In other words: Bring it on!

A shorter form:

Ave que vuela—¡a la cazuela!

Bird that flies—into the pot!

Ya comí, ya bebí, ya no me hallo aquí.

I ate, I drank, I am no longer found here.

A rather blunt way to announce your intention to eat and run. Slightly less offensive than a loud belch.

Después de un buen taco,
un buen tabaco

After a good taco,
*   a good tobacco*

A similar post-meal announcement, but this time signaling you are excusing yourself for a post-meal smoke.

Barriga (panza) llena, corazón contento

Belly full, heart content

This rapturous after-meal remark is somewhat informal (not for use at the embassy dinner, perhaps) but simple and expressive.

Reminiscent of the old English expression "The way to a man's heart is through his stomach" in that the same biological pathway is involved. But the Spanish phrase has none of the thinly veiled sexist connotation of the English one. All full bellies, regardless of gender, produce happy hearts!

Gracias por la flor; mañana vengo por la maceta.

Thanks for the flower; tomorrow I'll come back for the flowerpot.

It is common in social settings to be complimented—on your hair, your outfit, your figure. Compliments like this are informally known as *flores*, or "flowers." This expression is a cute way to acknowledge these compliments with a bit of humor, adding you'll be back for more!

El que mucho se despide pocas ganas tiene de irse.

One who says good-bye a lot doesn't really want to leave.

This is used toward the end of a meal or a party, for instance, when the Latino custom is to make the rounds and say individual good-byes to everyone in the room. If the good-byes take too long, it suggests the person leaving really would rather stay on awhile longer—and this expression is meant to encourage them to stay.

No te vistas, que no vas.

*Don't get all dressed up,
    'cause you're not going.*

The kind of thing a big sister will tell her younger sibling as she prepares to go out with her friends to the movies. Cinderella, for instance, probably heard this a lot. It's frequently used in a more figurative sense to signal (rather rudely) that the person being addressed is not being included in future plans. Ditto:

"Vamos" es mucha gente.

"Let's go" is a lot of people.

"Who said anything about '*We* . . .'?"

24. ¡Salud!

There is probably nothing that inspires the *dicho* maker more than a mug of beer, a glass of wine, or a shot glass of whatever-you're-having. *Dichos* and drinking seem to go together, and many a drinking establishment will reinforce this by displaying pithy sayings on its walls. Most of these encourage clients to keep drinking, of course, so their motives may be less poetic than financial. But it's still good to have a quiver full of wit handy when having a cold one.

Contra las muchas penas, las copas llenas;
  contra las penas pocas, llenas las copas

Against many sorrows, the glasses filled;
  against few sorrows, fill the glasses

Like many of the *dichos* in this section, this one is
a nicely rhymed linguistic invitation to drink and
drink some more. Here the logic is irrefutable: For
the drinker, there is never a bad time to imbibe. In
Mexico, you may hear this stated pithily as:

Para todo mal, mezcal;
  para todo bien, también

For everything bad, mezcal;
  for everything good, likewise

Mis dos razones para tomar mezcal:
porque sí y ¿por qué no?

My two reasons for drinking mezcal:
just because and why not?

More bullet-proof cantina logic.

Para el catarro, jarro; si es con tos, dos

For a head cold, a mug; if it's with a cough, two

Dichos convey much wisdom, and medical wisdom is
no exception. Here the diagnostic and dosage information are clear, although possibly not endorsed by
the A.M.A.

Need an excuse to go beyond two? Here's another
prescription:

Si tienes estrés, tómate tres.

If you're stressed, have three.

Con amor y aguardiente, nada se siente.

With love and aguardiente, you feel nothing.

Aguardiente, for those in need of an introduction, is a sugar-cane alcoholic drink that translates well as "firewater." Here love and drunkenness are compared, although it's not clear which is favored. At least drinking you can do on your own . . .

Toma del fuerte para que no sientas la muerte.

Have a sip of the strong stuff so you don't feel death.

This one is suitable for passing the flask in the trenches during wartime . . . or maybe at your local watering hole, just to add some drama to the ritualized after-work malted beverage.

P'arriba, p'abajo, al centro y pa' dentro

Up, down, to the center, and inside

This is the classic (verging on clichéd) toast to start a round of slurping and guzzling. It's often accompanied by complex movements of the hands up and down and other ritualistic movements reminiscent of "La Macarena."

For those with less energy, it's hard to go wrong with:

¡Salud!

Cheers!

Dios mío, si borracho te ofendo, con la cruda me sales debiendo.

Dear God, if drunk I offend you, with the hangover you end up owing me.

Alas, after a long night exhausting all the drinking *dichos*, the bill always arrives the next morning. And naturally there is a *dicho* for that as well.

Todo lo conserva el alcohol menos los empleos.

Alcohol conserves everything except jobs.

We learn at school that alcohol prevents decomposition and conserves specimens. Later in life, we may learn that it tends to have the opposite effect on employment. This *dicho* aims to lower the learning curve.

25. El pan de los pobres

As we've seen, there are *dichos* to warn us, instill us with wisdom, lift us up when we're down, and shake us when we grow complacent. Quite a few *dichos* talk to us about hope and looking ahead to a brighter day—even if, as several of these *dichos* suggest, chances may be slim to none that that day's ever going to arrive.

A cada capillita le llega su fiestecita.

Every little chapel gets its feast.

This *dicho* varies somewhat in meaning, depending on the context. At heart (and most often), it suggests "All things come to those who wait" or even "Every dog has its day." But it can also be used a bit ominously, as if the little chapel didn't really want its little feast. Parents, for instance, might say it in warning to try to straighten out their miscreant children: "Just you wait . . ." Maybe, in this latter context, the closest English equivalent is "What goes around, comes around"—for better or worse.

Algún día mi gato comerá sandía.

Someday my cat will eat watermelon.

A wistful way of saying, "Someday my luck will change for the better" or "Someday my ship will come in." What makes it amusing—or maybe really sad—is that the odds of your cat eating watermelon are probably pretty low, so if that's what it will take to signal a shift in your luck, you may be in for a long wait. Probably smarter to bet on the ship.

Día en que los chanchos vuelen, los olmos nos den sus peras y la tristeza su risa

The day that pigs fly, elms give us pears, and sadness its smile

These somewhat gloomy statements don't really belong in a section on "hope." To the contrary, they are basically saying your ship *ain't* coming in and your cat *ain't* gonna eat watermelon. Indeed, they are more or less placing the date of your lucky day right after the day hell freezes over. "Dad, can I borrow the car to go joy-riding with my underage friends?" "*El día que los chanchos vuelen . . .*"

Shorter but just as emphatic: *Cuando llueva pa'rriba*—"When rain falls up."

La esperanza es el pan de los pobres.

Hope is the bread of the poor.

Con pasteles de esperanza,
 nunca se llena la panza.

With cakes of hope,
 you'll never fill your belly.

Two oldies-but-goodies with distinctly incompatible views on hope. Suffice it to say that hope keeps a penniless person going, but at the end of the day, it won't meet your minimum daily requirements.

"Hoy es hoy y ayer se fue, no hay duda."

Today is today, and yesterday has gone.
 There is no doubt.

Not a *dicho* at all but a well-known line from a poem by Chilean poet Pablo Neruda, reminding us that hope is reborn with each new day.

La esperanza muere al último.

Hope dies last.

This is an extremely common sentiment and traditional *dicho* that encourages us all to live to fight another day. It comes originally from the Greeks and Pandora's box, where hope was the only thing left after all the evils of the world escaped. So that's what we're stuck with in the face of scourges, plagues, and plain ol' bad luck. Could be worse.

26. El karma

Alas, when all is said and done,
and ships have sailed or come in,
it's time to say some more—and
in *dicho* form—to commemorate
the event. For what are events but
learning opportunities, and what
are *dichos* but ways to make sure
we remember the lessons gleaned
from what we've just witnessed? In
this case, the theme is destiny, and
the lessons are our very essence and
how it changes—or never changes
at all.

El que nace pa' maceta del corredor no pasa.

*If you were born to be a flowerpot, you won't
make it out of the hallway.*

**El que nace pa' martillo del
cielo le caen los clavos.**

*For one who is born to be a
hammer, the nails will fall
from the sky.*

**El que nace pa' tamal del cielo le caen
las hojas.**

*For one who is born to be a tamale,
the leaves will fall from the sky.*

These are just a few examples of common "One who
is born . . ." *dichos*, all of which say that your destiny
is fixed at birth, for better or worse.

Aunque la mona se vista de seda, mona se queda.

Even if the monkey dresses in silk, it's still a monkey.

This traditional *dicho* is well understood by all age groups, more so probably than its equally traditional (and old) English equivalent: "You can't make a silk purse out of a sow's ear." In fact, in English nowadays you are probably more likely to hear "It's like putting lipstick on a pig," which says about the same thing: You are what you are, and slick packaging or fine fashion can't change your essence.

**El que es perico dondequiera es verde
(y el que es pendejo dondequiera pierde).**

*A parrot is green everywhere (and one who is a
shithead loses everywhere).*

This *dicho* works either in full or just as the first part.
Part one is straightforward enough: if you happen to
be a parrot, you're going to be green no matter where
you go. A.k.a. "A tiger can't change its stripes."

Part two is just an extension of the same principle
to losers, who lose wherever they go. It's probably
unnecessary to make the point, but it does add some
flourish, force, and, of course, a nice rhyme to the
sentiment.

Siembra vientos y recogerás tempestades.

Plant winds and you'll harvest storms.

From the Book of Hosea (8:7) in the Hebrew Bible:
"For they have sown the wind, and they shall reap the
whirlwind." Basically, this is something you don't
want to do: start a little bad something and have it
turn into a big bad something that spins out
of control.

Cría cuervos y te sacarán los ojos.

Raise crows and they'll gouge out your eyes.

For lack of a better example, think of the story (or folk myth) of the United States supporting Al-Qaeda to fight the Russians way back when . . . only to have them evolve in a distinctly unpleasant direction. Or, more prosaically, this *dicho* could apply when you hire and train someone who then turns backstabber and tries to steal your job.

El que la hace la paga.

He who does it pays for it.

Basic justice and just desserts: "Don't do the crime if you can't do the time," or "Don't roll the dice if you can't pay the price." Basic karma, comin' back to bite ya.

**Quisieron enterrarnos,
  pero se les olvidó que somos semillas.**

*They tried to bury us,
  but they forgot we are seeds.*

This is often called a Mexican proverb, although others attribute it to a Greek poet. It was reputedly a favorite incantation of the Zapatista rebels in Chiapas, Mexico, although I saw it most recently on a Democrats Abroad website. Everywhere it's a phrase used to revive and inspire the downtrodden. Words—and *dichos*—will set us free!

Illustrations: Jaime Zuverza
Design & typesetting: Dustin Kilgore
Typeset in Spectral by Production Type

Printed in the USA
CPSIA information can be obtained
at www.ICGtesting.com
CBHW061213181024
15831CB00013BB/44

9 781477 328637